Meet Your Bible

Meet Your Bible
AND DISCOVER LIFE

Branson L. Thurston, Ed.D.

 Abingdon Press

MEET YOUR BIBLE
AND DISCOVER LIFE

Copyright © 1997 by Abingdon Press

All rights reserved.

No part of this work may be reproduced or transmitted in any form or by any means, electronic or mechanical, including photocopying and recording, or by any information storage or retrieval system, except as may be expressly permitted by the 1976 Copyright Act or in writing from the publisher. Requests for permission should be addressed in writing to the Permissions Office, 201 Eighth Avenue South, P.O. Box 801, Nashville, TN 37202-0801; or call 615-749-6421.

This book is printed on recycled paper.

Scripture quotations in this publication, unless otherwise noted, are from the New Revised Standard Version of the Bible, copyrighted © 1989 by the Division of Christian Education of the National Council of the Churches of Christ in the United States of America, and are used by permission. All rights reserved.

ISBN-0-687-06540-2

03 04 05 06 — 10 9 8 7 6 5 4

MANUFACTURED IN THE UNITED STATES OF AMERICA

Art and Photo Credits: Cover and book design by Diana K. Maio; pp. 30, 47, 79, Gail Denham; pp. 31, 56, 68, 70, Israel Ministry of Tourism; p. 33, Marvin Jarboe; pp. 47, 57, 77, FPG International; pp. 55, 63, 72, © Norhill Photography; p. 64, Gene Plaisted; pp. 75, 76, Cleo Photography.

ACKNOWLEDGEMENTS

This book would not have been possible without the vision, support, suggestions, and efforts of many people. Steve Games, Duane Ewers, and Neil Alexander of The United Methodist Publishing House were willing to experiment with new ways of working and allocated time and freedom for me to write this book. Throughout the process, their questions kept the focus on the life-giving and transforming power of the Bible and on its relevance for the lives of youth today.

Danny Dixon, Joel Harbarger, Kim Oyler, Tracy Ritchie, Lois Runk, Tom Salsgiver, and Mike Selleck all contributed from their experiences and commitment to offer the best ideas possible. Although not all suggestions have been incorporated, the book is the stronger for those that were.

Susie Bonner, a dedicated Sunday school teacher, and John Page, director of youth ministries at Brentwood United Methodist Church, were generous with personal and class time in testing some of the ideas of this book. Lyndsay Howe served both as youth and adult in planning and implementing some of the sessions. Many other youth at Brentwood United Methodist Church in Brentwood, Tennessee, cooperated "above and beyond the call of duty" in trying out ideas and in offering suggestions for those that needed to be refined or dropped completely.

Once the book began to take shape, valued friends and colleagues at The United Methodist Publishing House made their unique contributions. Diana Maio contributed tirelessly her creative ideas as a designer. The critical eyes and editorial skills of Eric Skinner and Joy Thompson have been matched only by their compassion and concern for you who will read and use this book.

Finally, my wife, Betty, gave insight, encouragement, and support even when this effort demanded time that rightly belonged to her. This is yet one more instance of her contributions to my ministry—and my life.

While indebted to all of those mentioned above, I, as author, bear the responsibility for what finally appears on the printed pages. It is my prayer that you who read and use this book will truly *Meet Your Bible and Discover Life*!

Branson L. Thurston

CONTENTS

Introduction	**8**
How to Use This Book	**9**
Chapter 1: The WHY of the Bible	**11**
Chapter 2: The HOW of Meeting Your Bible	**16**
Chapter 3: The WHERE of the Bible	**30**
Chapter 4: The WHEN of the Bible	**41**
Chapter 5: The WHAT of the Bible	**54**
Chapter 6: The SO WHAT of the Bible	**66**

INTRODUCTION

The title states clearly what this book is all about. First, the resource is designed to help you *meet your Bible*. The deepest friendships often begin when a mutual friend arranges a meeting between persons who don't know each other very well. This book can function as a mutual friend to help you begin a relationship with the Bible. It is a relationship that will last a lifetime. It is a relationship that will help you celebrate in good times and that will stand with you and help you in bad times.

And Discover Life! There are many reasons people use the Bible. MEET YOUR BIBLE, like much of the Bible itself, urges you to look and listen for the *true life* God intends for you. The Bible helps us discover *life*. It is life that many people seek, but too many look for it in the wrong places and miss it. *True life* is discovered in relationship to God, the source of all life. The Bible is not a substitute for that relationship; it is a guide to help us discover and experience that relationship with God. The Bible helps us understand God's relationships with people through the ages—people who are very much like us, even though they may have lived in different places and may have worn different kinds of clothes. God acted in their times and lives, and God's presence made a difference. Their stories and experiences can help us see how God is acting in our lives and times today—and how God is offering us a relationship that leads to life.

The WHO Is the Story! The big questions for any story are *who, what, where, when, why,* and *how*. If you have looked at the Contents Page for this book, you probably noticed that there is no chapter on WHO. The reason is that the WHO of the Bible is the basis of every chapter in this book (and every book of the Bible, too). That WHO is God. In addition to WHO, there is also *who*. This who refers to us, people who have been created, loved, corrected, forgiven, and sustained by God. The story of the Bible is a story of God's relationship with people through the ages. It is a story that does not end on the last page of the Bible but that flows from the Bible into our lives today. As we read the Bible, we become part of the story of the people of God.

Remember: We Haven't Told You *Everything*! Surprise, surprise! This book does not deal with *everything* you will ever want to know about the Bible. As you use the Bible, you will discover fascinating people, important events, and awesome ideas we have not mentioned. This book simply aims to help you *begin* to use your Bible. The journey and relationship with the Bible will last your lifetime. Of course, you can never make the journey unless you take the first step. Let's get started!

Branson L. Thurston

HOW TO USE THIS BOOK

First, get ready to use MEET YOUR BIBLE with your Bible. There is one exception: If you do not own a Bible, you may wait until you have finished Chapter 2 before you buy one. Chapter 2 will help you decide on the Bible that will be best for you. It will help if you have a Bible for Chapters 1 and 2, so you may want to borrow one. By the time you begin Chapter 3, plan to use your own Bible. Otherwise, how can you meet the Bible without a Bible to meet?

Second, come prepared for interaction between MEET YOUR BIBLE and the Bible. There are different kinds of questions this book will ask you to consider. Some will ask you to *reflect*, some to *remember*, some to *imagine*, and some to *think*. All are intended to help you *meet your Bible*. As that meeting leads to a deeper relationship, you will begin to ask your own questions of the Bible. Those will be the best questions of all!

Third, learn to ask the right questions. There will be many important questions to ask, but some are more helpful than others. Dick Murray, in his book *Teaching the Bible to Adults and Youth* (Abingdon Press, 1993), suggests three questions that have proved helpful to many persons and groups involved in Bible study. These questions are *What does this passage tell us about God? What does this passage tell us about human beings (ourselves)? What does this passage tell us about the relationship between God and human beings?*

Fourth, use MEET YOUR BIBLE on your own or in a group. If you meet your Bible on your own, set aside regular blocks of quality time you can spend with MEET YOUR BIBLE and the Bible. Or you may already be part of a group that has decided to use MEET YOUR BIBLE. If the latter is the case, your journey has begun.

If you want to meet your Bible with a group, find someone you think will make a good leader and ask him or her to help lead the study. In many cases the leader will be an adult, but a youth can also lead. The leader will need to order the Leader's Guide and agree to spend additional time in preparation. A good leader will listen and move at the pace of the group.

Fifth, use MEET YOUR BIBLE at a pace that is most helpful to you. The best way for most will be to take your time and to do the reading and reflecting as suggested. Or you can rush it at a faster pace by skipping some of the suggested readings.

Sixth, use the "markers" in MEET YOUR BIBLE to get your bearings. Chapters 4, 5, and 6 use "markers" to help you meet your Bible. The markers deal with six major times or events in the life of the people of God in the Bible. These markers are there to give you an idea of "what's going on" when you read a passage from the Bible. Re-read Chapter 4's "fly-over" of the markers as you begin each remaining time or session after Chapter 4.

Seventh, try using some of the passages and reflection guides for your personal devotion time. You may find that some of the passages are helpful and that you want to build personal devotion time around some of the readings.

Eighth, try using the Bible as *your* book and *our* book. The Bible is indeed a personal book for *your* use, but it will mean more to you personally when you hear and read it as a member of the people of God. Watch and listen for how the Bible is used in your congregation. Ask your pastor how it shapes the order of worship. Listen for how psalms are used for praise. What does the Scripture reading say to you as you hear it? What does it say as the pastor interprets it? How do you interpret it? See if you can use the markers to get a firm sense of what is going on in the passage.

Ninth, do not try to master the Bible. Some people think that they can master the Bible just as they would Algebra 101. But the Bible masters us: There is always another insight and another inspiring discovery. Do not be discouraged by the difficult passages. Build on the passages that you find helpful; you will discover that there will be enough of those for a lifetime.

CHAPTER 1

The WHY of the Bible

Why Use the Bible?

You have already begun to answer that question. When you picked up MEET YOUR BIBLE and opened it to this page, it meant that in some way you are already aware that the Bible might be an important book for you. You may have a vague feeling, a strong conviction, or an idea that is somewhere between the two. But however clear or however fuzzy your impression, you sense that there just might be a good reason to use the Bible.

By the time you finish MEET YOUR BIBLE, you will have formed your own ideas about why the Bible is important. This very moment, you may have some interesting thoughts about why the Bible is an important book. Go ahead and write them down in the margins of this page or in the box below. No doubt you will discover new insights while getting to know your Bible; so when they hit you, write in the margins throughout this book (or in a separate notebook if you are a real neat-freak). Your notes will help you remember your thoughts and will be helpful to look back on in the future.

MEET YOUR BIBLE cannot give you all the answers, and it won't try to do so. But we do hope that this book can help you make some important discoveries of your own as you *meet your Bible*.

My Reflections

For All the Wrong Reasons

Lots of people have lots of reasons for using the Bible. Not all those reasons will help *you* meet your Bible and discover life. Some reasons that people have for studying the Bible may be a real turnoff; some study the Bible for the wrong reasons. You may even have your own "Top Ten List of Ways *Not* to Meet the Bible," but here are a few to consider:

1. For some the Bible seems to be a **Game Book**. They may work hard to see how many right answers they can have ready for their next game of trivia recall. Or perhaps the game may be to see how quickly persons or teams can find a passage ("Find Micah 6:8. Ready? Go!").

Now, we are not saying that you'll get zapped with lightning for playing those games. The games may even help you discover some things about the Bible. *It's just not the big reason for using your Bible.* You can play those games for years and never really meet your Bible.

2. Others use the Bible as a **Weapon**, *literally*. Even you may recognize the temptation. You find your younger brother or sister reading your diary or listening in on your phone call with someone special. The first thing you can grab is your Bible, and you . . . (We will let you imagine the rest of the scene.)

It's no surprise to you that the Bible was never intended to be such a literal weapon. For the record, however, it can help you deal with temptations and anger and relationships and lots of other things—including forgiveness for using the Bible as a weapon. (Even Moses lost his cool with those first stone tablets. Fortunately for his brother, Aaron, Moses broke them on the ground, not on Aaron's head.)

3. For some folks, an even greater temptation is to use the Bible as a **Weapon**, *figuratively*. They start with their own answers and then try to use the Bible to impose their answers on others. For instance, there was a time when people tried to use the Bible to enforce their own ideas about maintaining slavery. That approach reverses the order of things. We do not try to impose our answers on the Bible. Instead, our answers should be shaped and tested by our listening to the Bible.

4. Many may study the Bible as **Great Literature**. This approach is tricky, because it's not exactly wrong. Indeed, the Bible is great literature; and there is every reason to include it in any study of great world literature. *But it's still not the main reason for using your Bible.* A person can read—and enjoy—the Bible for years as great reading without ever really meeting the Bible.

Why? To Discover Life!

MEET YOUR BIBLE offers three good reasons to use the Bible. You may want to add others. The first is part of the title: to *Discover Life*.

A helpful clue to *Why use the Bible?* is to find out *why it was written*. For Christians, a good place to discover an answer is John 20:31. In concluding his Gospel, John tells why he wrote it. Here is how the passage appears in three versions (we will talk more about *versions* in the next chapter):

But these are written so that you may come to believe that Jesus is the Messiah, the Son of God, and that through believing you may have life in his name. (John 20:31, New Revised Standard Version)

But these are written so that you will put your faith in Jesus as the Messiah and the Son of God. If you have faith in him, you will have true life. (John 20:31, the *Contemporary English Version*)

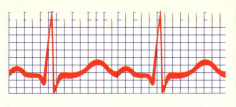

But these are written that you may believe that Jesus is the Christ, the Son of God, and that by believing you may have life in his name. (John 20:31, New International Version)

Looking at the Rest of the Bible Through John's Lens

John offers us a helpful lens to look at why the whole Bible was written. Every book of the Bible had (and has) its own reason and purpose, but few state that purpose as clearly as John's Gospel. What's more, when we look at the whole Bible down through the ages, we find that it has indeed led people to believe and to discover life.

Think About It
What is unique about a book that is written to help you *believe* or *to have faith that Jesus is the Christ*? How is such a book different from other kinds of books, such as

a driver's manual?

a sci-fi adventure?

an algebra book?

a sports star's autobiography?

a romance novel?

a science textbook?

the biography of a great President?

Jesus' Invitation to Nicodemus to Have Life
John is urging us to look deeper than a biological or literal meaning of "life." If you find it hard to get a grip on what that means, you aren't the first. Nicodemus had a hard time when he was thinking and talking about life on a literal and biological level, while Jesus was talking on a deeper and spiritual level.

Read about their conversation in John 3:1-16. How does Nicodemus keep missing Jesus' point about being born in a new way?

Eternal life means *now* as well as in the future. Jesus offered Nicodemus—and offers us—that which makes us truly alive. Reflect for a moment: Who do you know who seems more alive than others? It's more than breathing and a pulse that makes them alive! What is it?

When we read the Bible through John's lens, our eyes, ears, hearts, and minds are tuned to *believe* and to *have life*.

Why? To Discover Who We Are!
Have you ever been fortunate enough to be part of a large family reunion or a big family gathering for a holiday? a gathering of several generations? Or have you had an opportunity to talk with grandparents and to hear them describe family experiences down through the years? If so, you probably began to realize more about who you are. Our stories and relationships as families help us know who we are as persons.

The Bible is a book that introduces us to our spiritual family—and tells us who we are. In MEET YOUR BIBLE, especially in Chapter 4, we will see how the Bible is our family history as the people of God. Our family—the people of God—is a family with a long history. It is an extended family. Most of us are part of this family because of some adoptions along the way. As the people of God, we have family stories that have humor,

Meet Your Bible   AND DISCOVER LIFE

tragedy, hope, and guidance. As we get to know our family story—the story of the people of God—we discover who we are as children of God.

Why? As a Way to Live and Make Sense of the World!

When we discover the kind of life the Bible offers, we are offered a way to live in the world today. It makes a difference when we believe that this is God's world and that God is acting in the world today. The world seems quite different and we live differently if we think the world "just happened" or if we have never really thought about it being God's world.

The Bible opens a window that lets us see the world as God's world through experiences and writings of people who faced pain and joy, shame and glory, hope and despair.

Think About It

Reflect for a moment on what shapes your view of your world. What helps you make sense of it? Who or what helps you decide what is important to own and how you should spend your money?

Who or what helps you determine what is right and what is wrong? Who or what helps you decide whether you will do what you know is right or what you know is wrong?

These are fundamental questions that everyone faces; but not all of us probe deeper by asking, Who or what influences my answers to these questions? My family? television? friends at school? a whim?

Do I Trade My Tennis Shoes for Sandals?

When the Bible is part of your life, then you can begin to see the world biblically. Now, that does not mean trading your bike or car or wheelchair in on a camel or a donkey. You still live today! But God speaks through biblical events and biblical people to speak to you today.

If the Bible is part of your life and if you listen, the questions, the decisions, and the choices in your life will still be tough. (They were tough for biblical people, too.) But you will know you are not alone!

Also, when the Bible is part of your life, you will still have times when you know what the right choice is but end up doing the wrong thing. (Biblical people did that, too.) But the Bible has a lot to say about accepting consequences, receiving God's forgiveness, and making fresh starts.

Are you ready to Meet Your Bible and Discover Life?

CHAPTER 2

The HOW of Meeting Your Bible

A Personal Note About VCRs and Bibles

My family bought our first VCR for one reason: We wanted to watch (and listen to) tapes of our son's high school band. When we got that new VCR back home, I read the directions—several times. I tried to match various cables, inlets, and outlets on the diagrams with those on our VCR and TV. Eventually I had it all hooked up, and it worked! We put in the tape and got ready to enjoy the band shows.

In no time, all the buttons (PLAY, REC, REW, FF) made sense. And then we began to use other functions, like recording TV shows and playing rented movie videos. Although we had known that a VCR could perform such functions, they had not seemed that important at first. But now that we actually owned a VCR, we began to appreciate and enjoy many of the extra things it could do.

So What's the Point?

What does my VCR experience have to do with the Bible? *Think of this chapter as **A Basic Manual to the Bible**.* This chapter starts with the early steps of getting to know your Bible. It includes such helps as choosing the version you will use and how to use the contents page.

It's like the guide to that first VCR. Once you make the right connections, you begin to see what the machine can do. Once you can locate and use the PLAY, REC, REW, and FF buttons, you can access a variety of tapes and find the place you want within those tapes. To push the example further, you eventually will be pleasantly surprised to discover some special features that make your VCR more useful and more valuable.

Helpful Hints for the Next Step

Now let's move from VCRs to the Bible. Here are a couple of helpful hints to keep in mind as you read this chapter:

Helpful Hint 1:
Read what you need to read; "fast forward" through the familiar. If you come to information that is already familiar to you, scan quickly through that material and concentrate on the information that you need to help you meet your Bible.

Helpful Hint 2:
If you don't yet own a Bible, read this chapter before you rush out to buy one. This chapter will tell you some things about Bibles that can help you identify which version and what features will be most helpful to you.

What Is a Version?

If you look at the cover or the spine of most Bibles, you will find words or letters that tell you what *version* of the Bible you are holding. It may say something like New Revised Standard Version (NRSV), New King James Version (NKJV), New International Version (NIV), the *Contemporary English Version* (CEV); or it may indicate some other version.

Each version of the Bible has its own particular strengths. Select one or more versions in light of the strengths that are important to you. Generally, it is much better to have one (or more) of the versions that we will mention than to have a paraphrase.

A *Bible paraphrase* is a book (or passage) in which persons have tried to use their own words to say the same things that appear in one of the English versions. An *English version* is a translation into English from the language in which the Old Testament was written (Hebrew) and/or the language in which the New Testament was written (Greek).

When you are reading your Bible, it can be helpful to write your own paraphrase of a passage (write it in your own words). That's a good Bible study method. But when you are buying a Bible, generally you want a version—that is, a direct translation. When you (or your group) write your paraphrase, you are exploring the meaning of the passage for your own use. When you buy someone else's paraphrase, you may miss the opportunity to have the most accurate words for your own exploring of the Bible.

Why So Many Versions?

The Old Testament was written in Hebrew; the New Testament in Greek. (And both of them include some Aramaic, a variation of Hebrew that was spoken in Jesus' day.) A team of scholars can spend years translating a major version into a modern language such as English. One reason: There are often several good ways to translate the same Hebrew or Greek word or passage into English. (Imagine the discussions translation team members might have if they were trying to translate, "Dude, that's like, so bogus," into another language.) That's why having several versions available in a group can be helpful. Now let's look at some versions.

Meet Your Bible AND DISCOVER LIFE

Versions of the Bible: So What's the Diff'?

The **CONTEMPORARY ENGLISH VERSION (CEV)** was published in 1995 as a whole Bible. (The New Testament with Psalms and Proverbs was published in 1992.) *The major goal—and strength—of the CEV is the use of everyday English language so that it can be understood as easily as possible.*

Here is how the first two verses of Psalm 23 are translated:

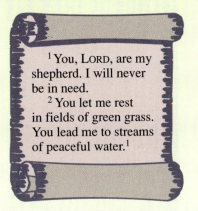

¹ You, LORD, are my shepherd. I will never be in need.
² You let me rest in fields of green grass. You lead me to streams of peaceful water.¹

And 1 Corinthians 13:12:

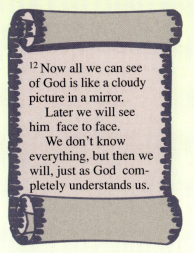

¹² Now all we can see of God is like a cloudy picture in a mirror.
Later we will see him face to face.
We don't know everything, but then we will, just as God completely understands us.

And two verses from Matthew 6:

⁵ When you pray, don't be like those show-offs who love to stand up and pray in the meeting places and on the street corners. They do this just to look good. I can assure you that they already have their reward.

⁹ You should pray like this:
Our Father in heaven,
help us to honor your name.

In 1976 the American Bible Society published another version with basically similar goals: **GOOD NEWS BIBLE: THE BIBLE IN TODAY'S ENGLISH VERSION,** sometimes referred to as the **TEV.** It remains a very usable Bible; but if you are buying a new Bible, the CEV is the more up-to-date choice of the two.

The **NEW REVISED STANDARD VERSION (NRSV)** was introduced in 1989. *The major goal and strength of the NRSV has been to maintain a balance between (a) modern English, (b) language that has rhythm and beauty for use in worship, and (c) the most accurate translation possible using up-to-date biblical scholarship.* Protestant, Roman Catholic, Orthodox, and Jewish scholars were involved in its translation.

Here is how the first two verses of Psalm 23 are translated:

And 1 Corinthians 13:12:

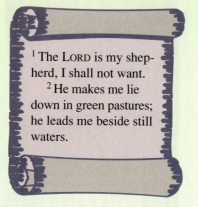

¹ The LORD is my shepherd, I shall not want.
² He makes me lie down in green pastures; he leads me beside still waters.

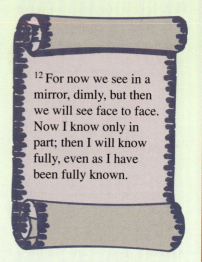

¹² For now we see in a mirror, dimly, but then we will see face to face. Now I know only in part; then I will know fully, even as I have been fully known.

And two verses from Matthew 6:

⁵ And whenever you pray, do not be like the hypocrites; for they love to stand and pray in the synagogues and at the street corners, so that they may be seen by others. Truly I tell you, they have received their reward.

⁹ Pray then in this way:
Our Father in heaven,
hallowed be your name.

The **REVISED STANDARD VERSION (RSV)** was published in 1952 and represented some of the best scholarship of that day. Like the TEV, the RSV is still a very usable Bible. (If you are buying a new Bible, the NRSV will be a more up-to-date Bible in terms of language, translation, and scholarship in general.)

The **NEW KING JAMES VERSION (NKJV)** was published in 1982. It is basically the work of Protestant scholars who wanted to be as faithful to the original language as possible. *The intent has been to maintain the beauty of the King James Version (KJV) while replacing obsolete words.*

Here is how the first two verses of Psalm 23 are translated:

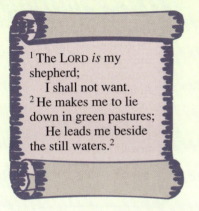

¹ The LORD *is* my shepherd;
    I shall not want.
² He makes me to lie down in green pastures;
    He leads me beside the still waters.²

And 1 Corinthians 13:12:

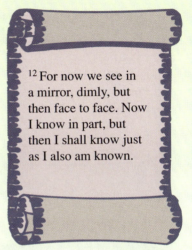

¹² For now we see in a mirror, dimly, but then face to face. Now I know in part, but then I shall know just as I also am known.

And two verses from Matthew 6:

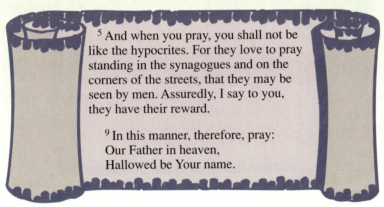

⁵ And when you pray, you shall not be like the hypocrites. For they love to pray standing in the synagogues and on the corners of the streets, that they may be seen by men. Assuredly, I say to you, they have their reward.

⁹ In this manner, therefore, pray:
Our Father in heaven,
Hallowed be Your name.

The **KING JAMES VERSION (KJV)** was published in 1611 and is still the favorite English translation of many people. It is the version from which most persons quote the Twenty-third Psalm and the Lord's Prayer. *For day-to-day use, however, most youth will find the NKJV to be more usable than the KJV.*

THE NEW JERUSALEM BIBLE (NJB) was published in 1985 and reflects the work of contemporary Roman Catholic scholars. Attention has been given to both beauty and clarity of language. It is the only major English version to use the Hebrew word *Yahweh* as the proper name for God.

Here is how the first two verses of Psalm 23 are translated:

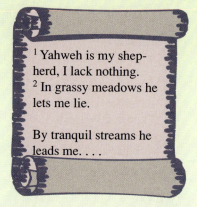

¹ Yahweh is my shepherd, I lack nothing.
² In grassy meadows he lets me lie.

By tranquil streams he leads me. . . .

And 1 Corinthians 13:12:

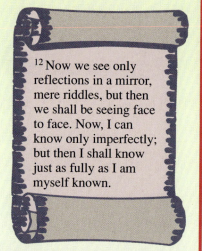

¹² Now we see only reflections in a mirror, mere riddles, but then we shall be seeing face to face. Now, I can know only imperfectly; but then I shall know just as fully as I am myself known.

And two verses from Matthew 6:

⁵ And when you pray, do not imitate the hypocrites: they love to say their prayers standing up in the synagogues and at the street corners for people to see them. In truth I tell you, they have had their reward.

⁹ So you should pray like this:
    Our Father in heaven,
    may your name be held holy.

The earlier **JERUSALEM BIBLE (JB)**, published in 1966, and the **NEW AMERICAN BIBLE (NAB)**, published in 1970, also reflect Roman Catholic scholarship. The NRSV, JB, NJB, and NAB all carry the *imprimatur*, indicating official approval of their use by Roman Catholics.

The **NEW INTERNATIONAL VERSION (NIV)** was first published in 1978 and has become a popular version, particularly among conservative Protestants. *It has tried to maintain the traditional tone of the Bible while translating words in ways that make them understandable to people in today's world.*

Here is how the first two verses of Psalm 23 are translated:

And 1 Corinthians 13:12:

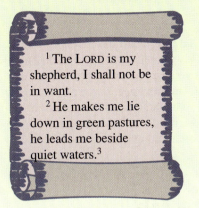

¹ The LORD is my shepherd, I shall not be in want.
² He makes me lie down in green pastures, he leads me beside quiet waters. ³

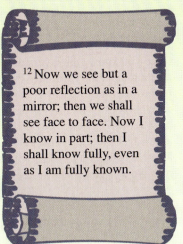

¹² Now we see but a poor reflection as in a mirror; then we shall see face to face. Now I know in part; then I shall know fully, even as I am fully known.

And two verses from Matthew 6:

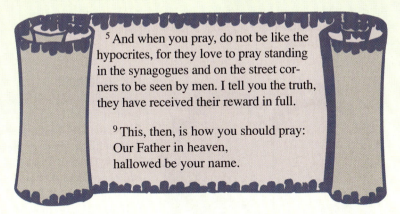

⁵ And when you pray, do not be like the hypocrites, for they love to pray standing in the synagogues and on the street corners to be seen by men. I tell you the truth, they have received their reward in full.

⁹ This, then, is how you should pray:
Our Father in heaven,
hallowed be your name.

Which Version Is Best for Me?

That decision is yours to make, but explanations and examples are provided in this chapter to help you make some choices. When scholars translate the Old Testament from Hebrew to English or the New Testament from New Testament Greek to English, there are times when no perfect translation is possible. All the above versions have used scholars who have tried to be as faithful as possible to the original text.

MEET YOUR BIBLE AND DISCOVER LIFE can be a companion to any of the versions indicated in this chapter. If you are using MEET YOUR BIBLE as a group, encourage the members to bring their different versions. Being able to check several versions can add to the richness of a Bible study, whether in a group or on your own.

Finding Your Way Inside the Book

Contents Page

Once you know which version you have, turn past the cover page and take a look at the **Contents Page**. This page lists the books of the Bible in the order they appear. It also tells you the page number for locating each book. It is not a sin to use the **Contents Page**. If you already know how to find every book of the Bible, congratulations! That can be a great time-saver. But don't feel guilty if you need to use the **Contents Page** to locate a book or a passage. The important thing is being able to find a passage that you want.

The Old and New Testaments

Most Bibles will have two major headings, **Old Testament** and **New Testament**, with a list of books under each heading. The word *testament* may also be translated as *covenant*, a word we will talk about in the chapters that follow.

Old Testament

Also called the **First Testament** or the **Hebrew Bible**, the **Old Testament** deals with the story of the Hebrew (later called Jewish) people and their relationship with God. We will discuss later the various types of literature in the **Old Testament**. Basically, the **Old Testament** comes from the Hebrew Bible, although the books are arranged in a different order.

By the time of Jesus, the **Hebrew Bible** had been translated into a Greek version, called the Septuagint. (Yes, they had different versions back then, too.) This was the Scripture most used by the early Christian church. It still is an essential part of the Christian Bible. Most of the New Testament assumes that readers are familiar with the **Old Testament**.

New Testament

This section of books deals with the life and teaching of Jesus, the birth of the church, and the spread of the Christian faith across the Roman Empire.

Apocrypha

Your contents page might have the heading **Apocrypha**, listed between the **Old** and **New Testaments.** The **Apocrypha** was written between 200 B.C. and A.D. 100. Roman Catholics consider the **Apocrypha** part of the Bible; Protestants generally regard it as helpful but not part of the Bible.

Cataloging the Library

The Bible is actually a collection of many books, so it really is a library. As with any library, it is helpful to classify the books under a few major categories or headings. After the **Old** and **New Testaments** (and sometimes **Apocrypha**), one way of organizing the books is found in the library on the next two pages.

WELCOME TO THE LIBRARY
Old Testament Wing

SECTION	BOOKS	SUBJECT MATTER
LAW (or Torah; also known as Pentateuch)	Genesis, Exodus, Leviticus, Numbers, Deuteronomy	Beginnings; God chooses a people for a mission and a covenant relationship; people given law for guidance.
HISTORY	Joshua, Judges, Ruth, 1 and 2 Samuel, 1 and 2 Kings, 1 and 2 Chronicles, Ezra, Nehemiah, Esther	People respond to God in both faithfulness and disobedience. People are given a king and become a great nation, but face disastrous consequences for their disobedience and injustice. Although God chastises for unfaithfulness, God remains ever faithful.
WISDOM (also known as Writings)	Job, Psalms, Proverbs, Ecclesiastes, Song of Solomon (Song of Songs)	Philosophical writings about big questions of life; songs of praise; prayers for God's help and guidance; songs of love.
PROPHETS		Messages of those called to speak boldly for God. Condemn the injustice and unfaithfulness of rulers and common people alike. Warn of consequences of disobedience of God's commands. Offer God's comfort and hope in times of deepest despair.
Major (Longer Writings)	Isaiah, Jeremiah, Lamentations, Ezekiel, Daniel	
Minor (Shorter Writings)	Hosea, Joel, Amos, Obadiah, Jonah, Micah, Nahum, Habakkuk, Zephaniah, Haggai, Zechariah, Malachi	

Meet Your Bible — AND DISCOVER LIFE

New Testament Wing

SECTION	BOOKS	SUBJECT MATTER
GOSPELS	Matthew, Mark, Luke, John	The life, ministry, and message of Jesus Christ.
HISTORY	Acts of the Apostles	The story of the birth of the church and of believers spreading the good news into all the world.
LETTERS (Epistles)	Romans, 1 and 2 Corinthians, Galatians, Ephesians, Philippians, Colossians, 1 and 2 Thessalonians, 1 and 2 Timothy, Titus, Philemon, Hebrews, James, 1 and 2 Peter, 1, 2, and 3 John, Jude	Letters to churches and to individuals, offering guidance, instruction, encouragement, and hope.
APOCALYPSE	Revelation	Coded message to Christians facing persecution; urges faithfulness in the face of persecution and offers assurance of God's final victory.

Chapters and Verses

Chapters and verses help us locate the passage we want in any Bible. Words can vary from version to version, and page numbers can vary widely from Bible to Bible. But chapters and verses remain the same.

When identifying a passage, the name of the book will usually be given first, the chapter next, and finally the verse. Thus, *John 3:16* refers to *verse 16* of *Chapter 3* of *The Gospel According to John*. If you see a lowercase *a* or *b* after a verse number, *a* refers to the first half of the verse and *b* refers to the second half.

A *hyphen* (-) means *through*; a *comma* (,) means *and*. (So *Psalm 23:1-4* refers to verses 1 *through* 4 of *Psalm 23*, while *Psalm 23:1, 4* refers to verses 1 *and* 4 of that same psalm.)

Time Out to Reflect

So far, we've been talking about "nuts and bolts"; and we will soon be talking about "bells and whistles." All of this is to *help you use your Bible*. Before we go further, relax, take a deep breath, and remember what the Bible is all about: life!

For this reflection time read Psalm 119:103-105 printed below from the NRSV. (Find and read the passage in your own Bible if you have it with you.)

> [103] How sweet are your words to my taste,
>   sweeter than honey to my mouth!
> [104] Through your precepts I get understanding;
>   therefore I hate every false way.
> [105] Your word is a lamp to my feet
>   and a light to my path.

For you personally, how well do these words apply to the whole Bible? Are the words of the Bible "sweeter than honey" for you? If not, how might that become true for you?

Now consider another symbol in the passage. Imagine walking along an unfamiliar trail in total darkness. It is a trail with numerous turns. Alongside the path are sharp, steep drop-offs. On the trail itself are various obstacles, such as exposed tree roots and rocks, which can easily trip a person. What would it mean to you to have a lamp (or other light) as you walk that trail? How is life like that path? How can God's word be like a lamp or a light?

Using Bells and Whistles in (or With) Your Bible

You can choose (or you may already have) a Bible with all the "bells and whistles." The term *bells and whistles* refers to those extra aids that are already included in your Bible. (These aids are sort of like extras on a new car—you can go with the standard model or you can get a Bible that's fully loaded.) If you choose a Bible that's standard, you can also purchase special helps separately in a variety of sizes and for a variety of prices. These special helps or accessories include *maps*, a *concordance*, a *Bible dictionary*, a *pronunciation guide*, and other resources.

Do not be overwhelmed by these extra helps if they are included in your Bible! They are a little like those extra gadgets and features on a new VCR. Most people record TV programs and watch movies on their VCRs long before they learn to work the other stuff. Likewise, you can start using your Bible well before you figure out how the bells and whistles operate.

If *maps* are included in your Bible, you will probably find different maps for major geographic areas at different periods in biblical history. (Names and boundaries changed with political events and fortunes.) We will talk more about maps in Chapter 3; but for now, if your Bible has maps, take time now to get acquainted with them. Maps can help give you a clearer picture of places and journeys. If your Bible does not have maps, you can use the ones provided in Chapter 3. If you plan to spend a lot of time on geography, you may want to purchase a *Bible atlas*.

A *concordance* lists alphabetically key words of biblical passages. Let's suppose a source of great comfort to you has been the verse, "The LORD is my shepherd, I shall not want." However, you aren't sure where to find it. You turn to a concordance for help and look under the key word *shepherd*. The concordance will have a long list of phrases from verses that contain the word *shepherd*. You look through the list and find the phrase you're looking for, "The LORD is my s., I shall not want." The concordance will then indicate the location in the Bible as "Ps. 23:1" (or maybe "Ps. 23.01").

If your Bible has a concordance, it will be a small one that contains only major listings of key words. You can buy a variety of separate concordances ranging from those offering selected major listings (under 200 pages) up to heavy-duty concordances that offer almost every listing (over 2,000 pages). If you buy a concordance, select one that matches your version of the Bible.

Some Bibles include a *dictionary*, an alphabetically arranged listing with definitions and descriptions of major biblical personalities, events, places, and themes. You can purchase separate *Bible dictionaries* that are larger and more extensive than the one that may be in your Bible. Some dictionaries will include a concordance with the dictionary.

Bibles may (and most dictionaries will) include a *pronunciation guide* to help you pronounce all those tricky names from Abednego (uh-BED-ni-goh) to Zerubbabel (zuh-RUHB-uh-buhl).

If a Bible indicates it is *annotated*, it will include study notes for passages you are studying. If a Bible indicates it is a *reference* (or a *cross-reference*) Bible, it will help you identify related passages. (For example, a reference Bible will indicate the source of an Old Testament passage that is quoted in the New Testament or where the same parable or event appears in another Gospel.)

Remember, the helps listed above are just that, *helps*. You can use your Bible with or without them.

---

[1] Scripture quotations on page 19 are from the *Contemporary English Version* Copyright © American Bible Society 1991, 1992.
[2] Scripture quotations marked "NKJV" are taken from the New King James Version. Copyright © 1979, 1980, 1982 by Thomas Nelson, Inc. Used by permission. All rights reserved.
[3] Scripture quotations on page 23 taken from the HOLY BIBLE, NEW INTERNATIONAL VERSION © 1973, 1978 by the International Bible Society, used by permission of Zondervan Bible Publishers.

CHAPTER 3

The WHERE of the Bible
(Setting the Stage)

WHERE You Live Affects WHO You Are

Think about how *where you live* affects your daily life, the things that you consider important, and the decisions you have to make. If you live in south Florida, you don't have to own a down-filled jacket, but you do need to know how to prepare for a hurricane. If you live in upstate New York, you do need that down-filled jacket, but you seldom worry about hurricanes.

In some places you celebrate every precious drop of water. In other places you fear the threat of too much water and the damage it can do. To someone living in the mountains of North Carolina, the world looks *and feels* quite different from the way it docs to someone living in the Arizona desert.

Bible Lands Are Part of the Bible's Story

Biblical people were also influenced by the land—sometimes by the land in which they lived and sometimes by the land through which they traveled. The land shaped symbols in their language and expressions in their psalms.

Knowing something about biblical lands can help us better understand experiences and messages of biblical people. As you read this chapter and look at its pictures, try to *feel* what it was like to live in their lands. And remember, while many boundary lines and place names have changed, many people still live in those lands today.

Where Is the Promised Land?
In the Heart

For the Hebrew people the *promised land* existed in two places. First and foremost, it was a place in the heart. In the hearts of the Hebrew people, it was God's promise that became their dream. It was real in their hearts before they settled the land, and it remained real in their hearts even when they were removed from the land.

Long after biblical times, black Christian slaves in America sang of the promised land as the promise of freedom. For many Christians today it is spoken of and sung about as a time when we will be united with God.

On the Map

Second, the *promised land* was a place in the world and on the map. On a map you can find it in the Middle East. It is where the southwestern part of Asia meets the eastern part of the Mediterranean Sea. Often it was called Palestine, but its boundaries and names would change with political and military events reported in the Bible. That is why we need several different maps for Bible study. (That should come as no surprise; names and boundaries continue to change even as we watch the evening news.)

Maps Help Tell the Story

Relax! Your relationship with God does not depend on your ability to read a map. But at times your Bible reading can be more enjoyable—and make more sense—when you can follow the action and locate places on a map.

We are going to start with a physical map of Palestine (on page 33). This is a map that will help us locate some key places, but it will help us with more than that. It will show us how high (and how low) the land areas rise and fall. From it we can also get an idea of areas that are likely to be green with vegetation and areas that are likely to be desert.

Great Variety in a Small Land

Although the land is small in area, it offers about as much variety as California: desert and mountains, coastal plains and river valleys, fresh water and salt water, arid land and farming land. Look again at the physical map to see how much variety you can find.

The next step will be to take a closer look at some key landmarks.

From Dan to Beer-sheba

"From Dan to Beer-sheba" is a phrase used a number of times to mark the northern and southern boundary cities. The distance from Dan to Beer-sheba is about 160 miles—if we measure it in a straight line ("as the crow flies"). Roads and rivers twist and turn, so road and river miles would be longer. Can you locate *Dan* on the map? (It's north and center on the map—almost due north of the Sea of Galilee.)

Now locate *Beer-sheba* on the map. (This city is south and slightly west on the map—due west of the lower third of the Dead Sea.)

Look more closely now at the two seas we have mentioned. The *Sea of Galilee* (also called *Sea of Chinnereth* in the Old Testament and *Lake of Gennesaret* and *Sea of Tiberias* in the New Testament) is a fresh-water lake, fed by the Jordan River. It played a prominent role in Jesus' ministry and teaching and in the lives of Peter and other disciples. Also note that this sea is 696 feet below sea level. (Yes, you read it right, the Sea of Galilee is *below* sea level.)

Look again, and notice how the *Jordan River* flows into the *Sea of Galilee* from the north and then flows out to the *Dead Sea* in the south. The actual distance between the two seas is about sixty-five miles; but the winding river never learned that the shortest distance between two points is a straight line, so its course is almost triple that distance. The *Jordan River* was an important boundary in a number of Old Testament events. For instance, Joshua and the Hebrews had to cross the Jordan to get to the Promised Land. In New Testament accounts, the Jordan River was where Jesus was baptized by John the Baptist.

Now look at the *Dead Sea* (or *Salt Sea*). It is 1296 feet *below* sea level, so you can see how the land drops as the Jordan flows from the north to the south. The *Dead Sea* at points has depths of another 1200 to 1300 feet. There is no river flowing out of the Dead Sea. The only water that leaves is by evaporation, leaving behind the chemicals that make the sea salty and dead to sea life.

Three Landmark Cities—Even persons who haven't read about them in the Bible, have heard stories and songs about *Jerusalem, Bethlehem,* and *Nazareth*. Let's take a closer look at these sites and find them on the map on page 33.

Jerusalem: Look west from the northern edge of the *Dead Sea* to find Jerusalem. Although in existence long before his time, David conquered and established Jerusalem as his capital city. We find it a center of religious and political life throughout the Old Testament. It was just such a center in Jesus' day. It was here he had major encounters with religious leaders. It was into Jerusalem that Jesus entered in triumph, celebrated a Passover meal in an upper room, and at his last supper prepared his disciples for his death. In Jerusalem, Jesus was tried and led through its streets to his crucifixion. Today it is a major religious city, not only for Christians, but for Jews and Muslims as well.

Bethlehem: Look about five miles south of Jerusalem and very slightly to the west, and you can locate Bethlehem. In the Book of Ruth, it is the town in which Ruth and Boaz met, married, and gave birth to Obed, who eventually became a grandfather to David. Luke's Gospel identifies Bethlehem as "the city of David," to which Joseph traveled with Mary for a census registration. While in Bethlehem, Mary gave birth to Jesus.

Nazareth: Now look north on the map about sixty-five miles north of Jerusalem. You can locate Nazareth almost midway between the Mediterranean Sea and the southern shore of the Sea of Galilee. Again, Luke's Gospel identifies Nazareth as the hometown of both Joseph and Mary. It was to Nazareth they eventually returned following the birth of Jesus. It was the town in which Jesus grew up. As an adult, he was often identified as "Jesus of Nazareth." In fact, it was Jesus who made Nazareth known to the world. There is no mention of Nazareth in the Old Testament.

How Many "Israels" Are There?

Just for fun, think about how many "Washingtons" there are. First, there's a fellow named George. Then there's the capital city (DC) of the United States. Many states have a town or city by the name of Washington; and, of course, there is the state named Washington. Sometimes on the news or in political talk, you hear folks use "Washington" to refer to the federal government.

In much the same way, you will find several uses for "Israel" in the Bible. Among those uses, the word can refer to

—*a person*,
—*a people*,
—*a united nation*, or
—*one part of a divided nation*.

The person is Jacob, who received "Israel" as a second name after a unique religious experience. From his children then descended "the Twelve Tribes of Israel." At times "Israel" can refer to all twelve tribes and their descendants. At other times (when some tribes were fighting other tribes), "Israel" can mean *some* of the tribes.

When David united the kingdom, it was often referred to as Israel. After Solomon's (David's son) reign, that kingdom was divided (around 922 B.C.), with the Northern Kingdom taking the name of Israel and the Southern Kingdom taking the name Judah. Even during that period and after the Northern Kingdom fell (in 722 B.C.), some prophets and writers still used "Israel" to refer to all the Hebrew people.

A Good Rule of Thumb (When Reading About "Israel"): First, if the passage is so specific that it is clear which definition of Israel the writer intends, then assume that definition. If it is less clear, then try as a definition *the chosen people of God* (the Hebrew people, the Jewish people). This is generally the meaning that is used in the New Testament and often in the Old Testament.

A Wide-Angle Lens on the Biblical Scene

So far we have "zoomed in" on the "Promised Land," the area that is often called Palestine. It is indeed the focal point of much of the biblical action. But there is a wider scene that is also very important to the Bible. That wider scene is reflected in some additional maps.

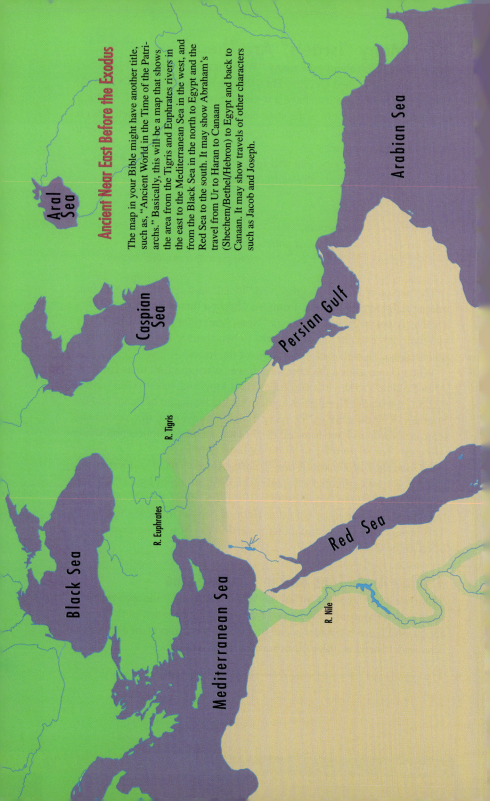

Ancient Near East Before the Exodus

The map in your Bible might have another title, such as "Ancient World in the Time of the Patriarchs." Basically, this will be a map that shows the area from the Tigris and Euphrates rivers in the east to the Mediterranean Sea in the west, and from the Black Sea in the north to Egypt and the Red Sea to the south. It may show Abraham's travel from Ur to Haran to Canaan (Shechem/Bethel/Hebron) to Egypt and back to Canaan. It may show travels of other characters such as Jacob and Joseph.

The Exodus

This map will show one or more possible route(s) of the Exodus from Egypt across the Sinai Peninsula to lower Canaan and around to the east of the Salt (Dead) Sea and up to Jericho. While this will be a tighter shot than "Ancient Near East..." on page 36, it will be a wider angle than Palestine.

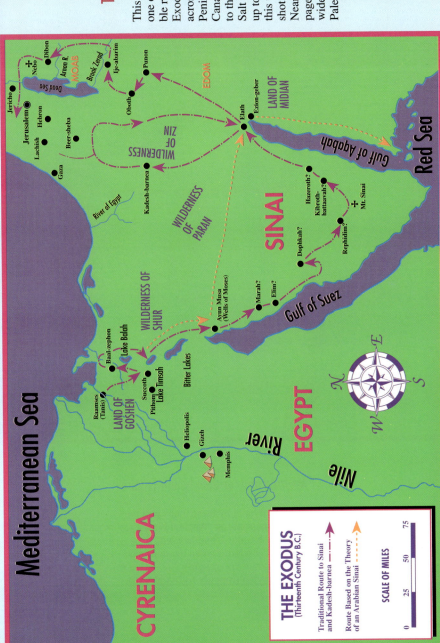

Adapted from *Bible Teacher Kit*, Copyright © 1994 by Abingdon Press.

Assyrian and/or Babylonian Empires

The area covered by these maps will be basically the same as "Ancient Near East Before the Exodus," but they will highlight boundaries when the dominant power was Assyria (roughly 722–612 B.C.) and/or Babylon (roughly 612–539 B.C.).

Time Out to Reflect

How do you react to the word *maps*? Is it with excitement (as vacation images come to mind)? Or is it with a "ho hum"?

Reflect back in time to early beginnings when God gave Abram (Abraham) a special mission and a special promise. It may not have been a vacation, but it was an invitation to begin an exciting journey. At one point, God told Abram

Look around to the north, south, east, and west. I will give you and your family all the land you can see. It will be theirs forever! . . . Now walk back and forth across the land, because I am giving it to you (Genesis 13:14-15, 17, CEV).

We, too, are invited to claim the lands of the Bible. That claim is based, not on holding a deed, but in awareness that in *real places* God has met and acted in the lives of our ancestors in the faith. God has met them on long journeys and in the quietness of one's own tent or home. God has met them when they were a great nation and when they were a conquered people in exile in another land. God has met them and continues to meet us in real places.

Read again and reflect on God's command and promise to Abraham. What promise do you hear as you meet your Bible and as you meet the lands of the Bible?

Map 1: *Ancient Near East Before the Exodus*—Wide-angle shot of the Middle (or Near) East from roughly 2000 B.C. through 1350 B.C. (Note that Jerusalem is slightly south and west of the center of the map.)

Map 2: *The Exodus*—Zooms in a little closer to show the traditional route of the Exodus (around 1350–1250 B.C.). Some scholars suggest other possible routes for the Exodus.

Map 3: *Assyrian and Babylonian Empires*—Pans out to show the Middle Eastern world when the dominant powers were Assyria (roughly 722–612 B.C.) and later Babylon (roughly 612–539 B.C.). Israel (the Northern Kingdom) was conquered and destroyed by Assyria in 722 B.C.; Judah (the (Southern Kingdom) was conquered by Babylon around 598–597 B.C. with the exile of leading citizens to Babylon at that time and in additional waves in 586 B.C.

Map 4: *Journeys of Paul*—A wide-angle shot again, but this time showing more of the western world and less of the eastern world than in Map 2 (note Jerusalem in the southeast corner of the map).

Look again at Map 3 and imagine that Israel and Judah were united as one kingdom. They were just such a united kingdom under King David. At that time the "Promised Land" would *roughly* have been about the size of present-day New Hampshire.

Jericho: Look a little west and a little north of where the Jordan flows into the Dead Sea, and you will find Jericho. Because of springs and precious water, Jericho is probably one of the oldest cities in the world. (There is evidence that it existed at least as early as 5000 B.C.)

CHAPTER 4

The WHEN of the Bible
(People on the Move)

What's the "Map" of Your Life, So Far?

In Chapter 3 we found that maps can help us understand the lands of the Bible. They help us "picture" relationships between landmarks, distances, journeys, and people.

Another kind of "map" can help us understand our own life stories. Take a few moments to think about the map of your life. (You may want to get two or three sheets of paper and a pen—or pens in several different colors if you are feeling creative.)

What four or five events have shaped your life and made you who you are right now? Use "markers" to indicate those events on your map.

Remember, this is *your* map; you can use hills and valleys, curves and detours, and/or straight, wide four-lane highways. Your map will probably look quite different from everyone else's.

Look at the "markers" on your life map. How have those events made a difference in who you are? in what you consider important? in what you hope or expect for the future?

A Map of the People of God

The Bible is one story, and it is many stories! It is true (as we discussed in Chapter 2) that the Bible is a library of many different kinds of literature and books. It is equally true that there is one story running through the whole Bible. **This common thread is the story of God's relationship with a people down through the ages.**

Just as the map of your life has "markers" that identify key experiences that have made you who you are, so there are "markers" that help identify key experiences that have made us who we are as the people of God. This chapter will help you identify six big markers in the life of the people of God. As you get to know your Bible better, you will discover other markers; but with these six you have the "markers" to help you establish your bearings to meet your Bible.

FLY-OVER MAP

There are several ways to explore new territory. (1) One way is to fly over the area to get the *big picture*. (2) Another way is to walk over the land, marking trails and identifying landmarks. (3) Still another way is to explore carefully one small area in detail.

This chapter will help you use the first two methods to explore the story of the people of God, and then you can spend a lifetime using the third to explore the Bible in depth. We begin with the "fly-over."

Marker 1 • THE DREAM
(The Journey Begins)
2000 B.C.: Abraham, Sarah, and a Promise

Marker 2 • BECOMING A PEOPLE
(The Greatest Camping Trip Ever)
1250 B.C.: Moses and Exodus

Marker 3 • A PEOPLE, A LAND, AND A NATION
(When the Act Was All Together)
1000 B.C.: David's United Kingdom

Meet Your Bible   AND DISCOVER LIFE

Marker 4 • THE PEOPLE FIND NEW HOPE; RELIGION FINDS NEW FORMS
(When Hebrews Became Jews)
586–538 B.C.: Exile and Return

Marker 5 • A PEOPLE WITH A MESSIAH
(Immanuel: God With Us)
4 B.C.– A.D. 30: Jesus

Marker 6 • A PEOPLE WITH A MISSION
(The Journey Continues . . . Into All the World)
The Christian Church

P.S.
Did you notice the blank circle with each marker? That space is for you to create your own symbol or icon that you think symbolizes that marker. While we have provided one icon, you may come up with one that is better for you—one that will help you remember that marker.

Take A Closer Look From the Ground

Now, it's time to explore the story of the people of God at the ground level. We will discover more details as we examine each marker a little more carefully.

Marker 1 • *THE DREAM*
(The Journey Begins)
2000 B.C.: **Abraham, Sarah, and a Promise**

In a Nutshell: Abram, whose father had already made one long move, was called by God to travel to yet another distant land. God promised Abram that he and his heirs would be a great nation and a great people—a blessing to "all the families of the earth." Abram and his wife, Sarai, responded in faith and began the long journey. At times they doubted God's promise, and at times tried to take matters into their own hands; but God maintained a close relationship with them. God secured the relationship in a special agreement, a *covenant*. In establishing the covenant, God changed Abram's name to *Abraham* and Sarai's to *Sarah*.

IF YOU WANT TO EXPLORE FURTHER, here are some passages and questions to help you:

Where had Abram's family settled?
Where had they started from?
(Look at a map and determine roughly how far they had traveled.)
- Genesis 11:31-32

What did God call Abram to do?
What did God promise Abram?
- Genesis 12:1-3

Where did Abram go? Roughly what was the distance?
- Genesis 12:4-8

Reflection Questions:

What would travel have been like around 2000 B.C.? What would it have been like to travel the distances that Abram traveled? What do you *imagine* Abram and Sarai gave up to follow God's call?

Meet Your Bible AND DISCOVER LIFE

Marker 2 • BECOMING A PEOPLE
(The Greatest Camping Trip Ever)
1250 B.C.: Moses and Exodus

In a Nutshell: In time, Abraham's grandson Jacob became head of the tribal family. Jacob received the name *Israel*. One of Jacob's (or Israel's) sons was *Joseph*. Overcoming many obstacles, Joseph responded faithfully to God and achieved a high position in the court of the Egyptian pharaoh. Joseph assured the survival of his tribal family (children of Israel) by bringing them to Egypt during a famine.

As more time passed, Joseph died and eventually another pharaoh (or king) came to the throne. This new pharaoh did not know of Joseph; but he did consider the people of God to be a problem, so he made them slave laborers to the Egyptians. By now the people of God were sometimes called *Israelites* and sometimes *Hebrews*.

God called Moses to lead the Hebrews to freedom and to help fulfill the promise made to Abraham. After several broken promises from Pharaoh, God directed Moses to lead the people out of Egypt and into the Promised Land. The escape from Egypt was dramatic and the journey to the Promised Land a long one that took many years.

On that journey God took care of the people in miraculous ways, but they often found it difficult to be faithful to God. At one point they declared they would rather have the security of their former slavery than endure the risks of the journey. Even as Moses was on Mount Sinai receiving God's directions for the people, the distrusting and impatient people made and worshiped a golden calf.

Despite the people's unfaithfulness, God established the covenant with them at a new and deeper level. God's law was now pivotal to the people's relationship with God and with one another. The Israelites emerged from the wilderness experience not only with law and covenant, but also with a greater sense of identity as a people. (A long, hard camping trip is a great way to get to know one's family!)

IF YOU WANT TO EXPLORE FURTHER, here are some passages and questions to help you:

How were the Hebrews freed from slavery in Egypt?
What did God expect from the Hebrew people?
- Joshua 24:4-13 (This summary, given by Joshua after the Hebrews arrived in the Promised Land, leads up to the renewal of the covenant with a later generation.)
- Exodus 20:1-21

Even while they were still in the wilderness, how difficult was it for the people to remain faithful to God? What did God do?
- Exodus 16:1-21
- Exodus 31:18–32:1-14

Reflection Questions:

Can you recall some times in your own life when you have found it difficult to trust God? Are there some other things that you found easier to trust than God? What are some things that have been (or might be) idols for you?

Marker 3 • A PEOPLE, A LAND, AND A NATION
(When the Act Was All Together)
1000 B.C.: David's United Kingdom

In a Nutshell: The people entered the Promised Land (Canaan) under Joshua's leadership. For years there were skirmishes over the land. Battles and hardships were often linked with the people's unfaithfulness; victory seemed to come with faithfulness. A series of leaders, called *judges*, responded to God's call at crucial times to lead the Israelites to faithfulness and victory.

Over time, the land was secured and God granted the people's desire to have a king. The second king was David, who made the people into a great nation, respected by other nations. Although David had his faults and sins, he struggled to be faithful to God and to keep the nation faithful to God. David did not see himself as a god, as some kings did. Rather, he listened to God's prophets, who advised and corrected him. God's promise to Abraham seemed to find fulfillment under David. Down through the ages, David became the symbol of the ideal ruler and his kingdom the symbol of the ideal kingdom. That symbolism and imagery of David's rule and kingdom are important to the New Testament.

David's son Solomon had the Temple built in Jerusalem. Solomon brought greater wealth and acclaim to the kingdom. That "success," however, was costly in terms of the burden it placed on the people and the loyalty the people felt toward the king. Upon Solomon's death the nation was divided into the Northern Kingdom of Israel and the Southern Kingdom of Judah. Around 722 B.C., Israel fell to the brutal Assyrian Empire. If God's mission would ever be fulfilled, then Judah, with Jerusalem as its capital, had become the best hope.

IF YOU WANT TO EXPLORE FURTHER, here are some passages and questions to help you:

Over what land(s) did David rule?

Why is it called a "united kingdom"?
- 2 Samuel 5:1-5

What was the capital city of the kingdom? By what names was it known?

Why was David considered a great king?
- 2 Samuel 5:6-10

How did David view his relationship with God? the nation's relationship to God?
- 2 Samuel 7:18-24

Reflection Questions:
Can you recall a time in your life when everything seemed to "come all together just right"? If so, how did you express your joy? How did you express your thankfulness? What, if anything, brought an end to that "all together" time?

Chapter 4   The WHEN of the Bible   47

Marker 4 • THE PEOPLE FIND NEW HOPE; RELIGION FINDS NEW FORMS
(When Hebrews Became Jews)
586–538 B.C.: Exile and Return

In a Nutshell: Prophets like Isaiah and Jeremiah warned Judah to learn from the Northern Kingdom's mistakes and fate, but many people and some rulers failed to put their final trust in God. By 597 B.C., Babylon had become the power of the Near East, had conquered Assyria, and was demanding tribute from Judah. Despite Jeremiah's warnings, those who held power in Jerusalem resisted Babylon's demands. At first Babylon took the king and other top leaders into exile in Babylon (in 597 B.C.). With each display of resistance, Babylon took sterner and sterner measures. Finally, around 586 B.C., Babylon destroyed Jerusalem and carried even greater numbers of the leading citizens into exile.

Babylon was not as brutal as Assyria had been. Hebrews taken into exile were permitted to own land, build homes, and even hold minor political offices. The greatest threat to the Hebrews was remaining faithful to God in a distant land that offered its own attractive gods. It was tempting to adopt Babylonian ways and to wonder if the gods of the victorious Babylonians were more powerful than the God of the conquered Hebrews.

Jeremiah and other prophets urged patience, hope, and faithfulness. Jeremiah told of a *new covenant* that God would offer the people of God; it would be a covenant written *upon their hearts.* Many believe that during the Exile, committed Hebrews found the occasion to organize their sacred writings and to establish religious practices and institutions that enabled them to remain faithful to God. It is at this point that many begin to refer to the people as Jews.

Meet Your Bible — AND DISCOVER LIFE

In 539 B.C., Babylon was conquered by Persia. The next year, the Persian king Cyrus permitted those Jews who wanted to return to Judah to do so. Those who chose to return had to meet the challenge of rebuilding the Jerusalem walls and the Temple, important steps to restoring the nation.

Those Jews who remained in Babylon became part of the *dispersion* or *diaspora* (Jews dispersed outside the land of Palestine). For various reasons, including trade, there were also Jews dispersed to Egypt and other lands around the Mediterranean Sea.

IF YOU WANT TO EXPLORE FURTHER, here are some passages and questions to help you:

Why was King Jehoiachin considered a bad king?
What happened to his kingdom?
- 2 Kings 24:8-17

Why was King Zedekiah considered a bad king?
What happened to his kingdom? What was destroyed?
- 2 Kings 24:18–25:12

Roughly, how far was it from Jerusalem to Babylon?
What was it like to live in exile in Babylon?
- Psalm 137:1-6 (the bad news)
- Jeremiah 29:1-8 (the good news)

How was the NEW covenant going to be different from the original one?
- Jeremiah 31:31-34

Reflection Questions:
If you had been carried into exile, what would have been most difficult for you? What would have been your greatest temptations? What would have given you hope?

Marker 5 • A PEOPLE WITH A MESSIAH
(Immanuel: God With Us)
4 B.C.–A.D. 30: Jesus

In a Nutshell: Around 333 B.C., the Greeks conquered the Persians. In turn, the Greeks were conquered by the Romans around 146 B.C. By the time of Jesus' birth, the dominant political and military power was Rome. Greek culture, however, continued to exert a strong influence throughout the empire. Greek philosophy and language influenced the ways first Jews and then Christians expressed ideas and transmitted their sacred writings.

For the most part, Rome allowed the Jewish people freedom to worship and practice their religion *as long as their activities did not "make waves" for Rome*. Anytime it appeared that might happen, Rome was likely to tighten its grip. There were daily reminders that the land was controlled by Rome. (For example, a Roman soldier could require a person to carry his pack for one mile [Matthew 5:41].)

Many Jews longed for the independence and status that the nation had enjoyed in the days of David's rule. Many wondered if God's promise to Abraham would ever be fulfilled. Many hoped for a leader, an "anointed one" (or *messiah*), who could restore the people and the nation to the prominence they had held under David.

Into this setting, Jesus Christ was born. (*Christ* is the Greek word for *messiah*.) In Jesus, God came into human flesh and life. Jesus did not fit the typical image of a mighty king, although Joseph (Jesus' earthly father) was a descendant of David's. Joseph and Mary were neither wealthy nor powerful but were typical village people from Nazareth in Galilee. Nazareth was a far cry from the city of Jerusalem, the center of religious and political life.

As an adult, Jesus appeared to be more of a teacher than a king. While he did talk of a Kingdom, it was different from Rome's rule—or even David's earlier rule. It was not earthly in that sense, and yet Jesus' followers could become part of it *now*! The Kingdom was, is, and will be one over which God reigns. The Kingdom is built on love and humility rather than power and might.

Jesus called disciples to follow him and to learn more about the Kingdom. But Jesus did more than welcome a few disciples. He forgave sinners and welcomed other unacceptable people into the Kingdom. This angered many religious leaders who had their own narrow definition for what was necessary for a relationship with God. They feared that this "carpenter from Nazareth" would destroy the law upon which their religion was built.

Jesus declared that he had come to *fulfill the law*, not to destroy it. Just as Jeremiah had spoken of a new covenant that would be engraved on the heart, so Jesus talked in terms of *the spirit, rather than the letter*, of the law.

Besides those who saw Jesus as a threat to their religious authority, there were others who feared Jesus as a political threat. And there were yet others who were upset because Jesus did not exercise the power they expected of a messiah.

Several parties conspired to get rid of Jesus. After a mockery of a trial, he was executed on a cross. His discouraged disciples were shocked and amazed when God raised—*resurrected*—Jesus from death. He appeared several times to the disciples and directed them to continue his mission and ministry until his return. He promised they would receive the power of the Holy Spirit that would enable them to be his "witnesses in Jerusalem, in all Judea and Samaria, and to the ends of the earth" (Acts 1:8).

IF YOU WANT TO EXPLORE FURTHER, here are some passages and questions to help you:

Where did Jesus come from?
What does it mean to you for the Word to become flesh and live among us?
- John 1:1-18

What is Jesus' attitude toward the law?
What are his expectations of us?
- Matthew 5:13-20, 43-48

How does Jesus reflect the "new covenant" that Jeremiah described?
- 2 Corinthians 3:1-6

Why did Jesus upset many of the religious leaders?
- John 5:1-18

What were the consequences of Jesus' conflict with religious leaders?
What was the final outcome?
- Luke 23:13-25
- Luke 24:1-3, 13-35

Reflection Question:
How would your life be different if you took Jesus' message seriously?

Marker 6 • A PEOPLE WITH A MISSION

(The Journey Continues . . . Into All the World) The Christian Church

In a Nutshell: A few weeks after Jesus' resurrection, Jews gathered in Jerusalem to celebrate the festival of Pentecost. Because the dispersion had continued since the days of the Exile, the Jews had come from many nations and spoke many languages. As Jesus had promised, the Holy Spirit enabled the disciples to speak of God's mighty acts. Many were amazed that all persons heard the message in their own tongues. This event is often called the birthday of the church.

New followers responded to the preaching and teaching of the disciples. The original disciples and followers were Jews. They met regularly at the Temple and often won new followers there. Some of the Jewish leaders began to feel that the disciples and the message about Jesus Christ were a threat to established institutions and teachings. The disciples were ordered to stop teaching about Jesus and to stop healing people in his name. The disciples and other new followers continued to proclaim their message. The Jewish leaders began to arrest and imprison followers of Christ. As the persecution increased, Stephen was stoned to death (an official means of execution) for speaking out for his faith.

Present at Stephen's death was Saul, a young man well trained in the Jewish law. Saul not only approved of Stephen's execution, he also actively arrested and jailed many followers of Christ. Saul asked for and received official permission to go to Damascus and arrest persons there who were followers of the *Way* (what Christians were first called). As Saul drew near Damascus, he was dramatically confronted by the risen Lord and was converted as a follower of the Lord's Way. Saul's name was eventually changed to Paul, and he became a powerful preacher and missionary.

On his three missionary journeys, Paul established churches across Asia and into Macedonia (Greece). His final travel took him to Rome. His letters to churches were the earliest writings to become part of the New Testament.

Although relationships were strained between themselves and the Jewish leaders, the followers of the Way continued to live as Jews. They went regularly to the Temple; and when not in Jerusalem, they went to a synagogue. They believed it was important to observe such Jewish practices as abstaining from food (such as pork) that was considered unclean. Since the days of Abraham, it was necessary for all male Hebrews or Jews to be circumcised as a sign of the covenant. Normally, this was done while the boy was an infant. If a *Gentile* (a person who was not a Jew) wanted to convert to Judaism, it was necessary for him to be circumcised.

Meet Your Bible   AND DISCOVER LIFE

God led Peter to see Gentiles in a different way and to baptize a Roman military officer (Cornelius) and his household. Paul and Barnabas were also winning even greater numbers of Gentiles. This posed a tough question: Was it necessary for Gentiles to be circumcised as Jews before they could become Christians? A council of the church was called in Jerusalem to answer that question. After lengthy debate, Peter, Paul, and Barnabas convinced the council not to place such a painful requirement on the Gentiles. Those present still thought of themselves as loyal Jews, but that decision set Christianity on its own course as a religion.

IF YOU WANT TO EXPLORE FURTHER, here are some passages and questions to help you:

What did Jesus commission the eleven disciples to do?
- Matthew 28:16-20

What did Jesus promise his apostles?
- Acts 1:1-5

How was Jesus' promise fulfilled?
- Acts 2:1-17, 43-47

Who was Stephen and why was he killed?
- Acts 6–7

What caused Paul (Saul) to change from persecutor of Christians to Christian missionary?
- Acts 9:1-31

Why did Peter begin to include Gentiles?
- Acts 11:1-18

How did the church decide to deal with Gentiles who wanted to become Christians?
- Acts 15:1-21

According to Paul, what is necessary to put us in a right relationship with God?
- Galatians 3:1-14

Reflection Questions:
Has God called you to reach out to someone whom others consider "different" or "unacceptable"? How can you help persons discover that God already loves them?

CHAPTER 5

The WHAT of the Bible

The "markers" we used in Chapter 4 help us remember how God acts in the lives of people and in the events of history. The markers can help us know "where we are" in the story of the people of God when we read the Bible.

We use those same markers in this chapter, but this time to help us look at some of the big ideas we can discover in the Bible. When people meet God, they no longer see themselves or the world in the same way. Ideas are a way of talking about those encounters with God and about our relationships with God today.

These ideas are presented to help you get started. As you continue to use your Bible, you may find your own words that better express the ideas for you. In fact, you may find yourself changing the words several times during your life. That's OK! We are always trying to stretch our words to help us talk about God, who is greater than any words can express.

Marker 1 • THE DREAM
(The Journey Begins)
2000 B.C.: Abraham, Sarah, and a Promise

Covenant: An "agreement" that God offered the people of God. While mentioned earlier in Genesis, it takes on a special form with God's promise to Abraham to make the people into a great nation (or many nations) and to watch over the people. The people's agreement to remain faithful to God would be symbolized by the circumcision of all Hebrew males.

Under Moses (Marker 2), God gave the people the Law as guidance for their relationships with others and with God. Obedience to the Law became one way the people kept the covenant.

Time after time throughout the Bible the people failed to keep the covenant. Because the people failed to keep their part of the agreement,

God could have abandoned or even destroyed them. Instead, the loving God offered the people opportunities to renew the covenant and to keep the special relationship.

Marker 2 • BECOMING A PEOPLE
(The Greatest Camping Trip Ever)
1250 B.C.: Moses and Exodus

Chosen people: God chose a special people for a mission and a purpose. The idea was implied in God's dealings with Abraham, but it was stated in greater detail in God's dealings with Moses. As God prepared the people to enter the Promised Land, God warned Moses that the people must remain faithful. God declared to Moses that the people are chosen. (See Deuteronomy 7:6-11.)

Covenant (See Marker 1)

Law: Guidance for conduct of the people of God. *Torah* is the Hebrew word for Law; it can also be translated as "instruction." If you have ever been in a confusing situation where no one was sure of what was right and what was wrong, you can appreciate the words of the psalmist, who could declare that those who are happy are those whose "delight is in the law of the LORD, / and on his law they meditate day and night" (Psalm 1:2). The basic Hebrew view was to receive the Law as a gift.

A point of minor confusion: In addition to the above reference, there are places where the Bible speaks of law in the narrow sense of specific laws of Moses; at other times it broadly refers to the first five books of the Bible.

Chapter 5 — The WHAT of the Bible

Priest: One who officiates at the altar and who mediates between the people and God. For the Hebrews, Moses' brother Aaron was the first priest. Aaron's male descendants were to form the priesthood for the Hebrew people. The priests also had responsibilities for teaching the people about the Law.

Sacrifice: In mediating between God and the people, the priests offered sacrifices at the altar as a sign of the people's repentance and desire for a restored relationship (atonement) with God. Often the sacrificial offerings were cattle, sheep, or goats that were without blemish. (You would not offer something imperfect to God.)

Marker 3 • A PEOPLE, A LAND, AND A NATION
(When the Act Was All Together)
1000 B.C.: David's United Kingdom

King: The ruler of a nation. As indicated in Chapter 4, even though David was the second king over the Hebrew nation, he was remembered as the greatest king. He tried to be faithful. When he did sin, he realized that he owed obedience to God. For many neighboring nations, their king would claim to be a god. Not so for the Hebrews, who affirmed that God ruled over the king. David recognized that he ruled *under God and God's Law* (Torah). Not all kings recognized that accountability.

A point to keep in mind: Because the king symbolized one of the most powerful figures in their experience, the Hebrew people sometimes used that symbolism in referring to God as King. See Psalm 24:7-10 for an example.

A point to reflect on: Is there anyone in your experience who symbolizes what a king did in the Hebrew experience?

Today some royal families are almost ridiculed by tabloids—even in their own countries. Many kings and queens are subject to a parliament or council. The President of the United States is accountable to the Constitution, shares power with Congress and the Supreme Court, and is accountable to the voters. None of these restrictions applied to a typical Middle Eastern ruler in David's day. A king *had the power of life or death* over anyone who challenged his authority.

Prophet: A person who spoke for God and who spoke out for God. Predicting the future was NOT at the top of the list on the job description of most biblical prophets. They spoke out for God to remind kings, religious leaders, and common people alike that they all were subjects of God and must live under the Torah. The people and their leaders were to trust and obey God and show justice toward others. When prophets did deal with the future, it was often in terms of "*IF* you (or the nation) continue doing that which is evil, *THEN* there will be consequences to pay." Another way prophets talked about the future was to offer God's hope in times of despair. Some offered assurance that God would have the final say and that God's people would survive, perhaps under a special leader whom God would provide.

God called prophets from all walks of life and all social groupings. Some had the social standing and graces to fit into the palace scene. Others were hard-working people, more comfortable working in fields and vineyards than in the royal court. Whatever their station, they responded to God's call and risked speaking out for God when called.

REFLECTION TIME: *Power Play*

Remember the power a king could exercise. Remember the calling that drove a prophet to speak out for God. Now read the story about King David and Nathan the prophet in 2 Samuel 12:1-14. Imagine the scene: After David committed adultery with Bathsheba, she became pregnant. David tried to conceal what he had done by arranging to have Bathsheba's husband, a soldier named Uriah, brought home for a couple of days. David thought that Uriah would later assume the child to be his own. But Uriah was a true and loyal soldier who would not sleep in his own bed while his fellow soldiers were in tents and preparing for battle. David then arranged for Uriah to be put in the front lines of battle where he was sure to be killed—and indeed he was.

David had coveted (desired) his neighbor's wife, had committed adultery, and had killed Uriah. He had broken at least three specific commandments. In terms of the broader spirit of Torah, he had lied, cheated, misled people, and used his power in unjust ways.

For some nations the response would have been, "The king can do no wrong; he is above the law and can do whatever he pleases." David still had the power of life or death over anyone who challenged him. Imagine what it was like to be Nathan the prophet confronting the king for his sin. (Also imagine the thought Nathan must have given to how he would confront the king.) Imagine what it was to be like David responding to Nathan's story.

The biblical understanding was that God was the true ruler. David (and every other king) was expected to be as just, obedient, and faithful as any other Hebrew.

P.S.: *Another Kind of Power Play*

Remember the priests we met under Marker 2. They were responsible for performing sacrifices and other rituals. Detailed rules described how rituals were to be observed both by priests at altars and in the Temple and by people in their homes. When people and leaders thought they could please God just by doing the rituals, prophets like Amos challenged them to be faithful and obedient in a far deeper sense. Read Amos 5:21-27 to see what Amos had to say to those who were more concerned about rituals than justice. This is but one of many examples of prophets challenging other religious leaders as well as religious practices.

Justice: Fairness in how one deals with others. Justice goes deeper than the letter of the law; it is concerned with fairness to others, no matter what their station in life. It is the spirit behind Torah. As Nathan demonstrated by the story he told David, the king was expected to be just. Throughout the Old Testament are reminders of justice for widows, orphans, and others who were more vulnerable than others. Prophets frequently reminded the people of God that the health of the nation and the people depended on their being just and acting out of justice.

Mercy: Kindness and compassion that goes beyond what is required. Time and again, when the people broke the covenant, God could have ended the covenant relationship with them. Instead, God showed mercy by going beyond the agreement and renewing the offer for the special relationship. In turn, the people and the nation were expected to show mercy to others. The prophet Micah summed up God's expectation of God's people:

> What does the LORD require of you?
> To act justly and to love mercy
> and to walk humbly with your God.
> (Micah 6:8, NIV)[1]

Marker 4 • THE PEOPLE FIND NEW HOPE; RELIGION FINDS NEW FORMS
(When Hebrews Became Jews)
586–538 B.C.: Exile and Return

Dispersion: Jews who were scattered from Palestine to other places throughout the world. For most this came about when Babylon conquered Judah and took the leading citizens into exile in Babylon. Others fled to Egypt and other nations to avoid being forced to go to Babylon. Even before and after the Exile there were Jews who moved and settled across much of the Mediterranean world for purposes of trade and commerce. Jews in dispersion and in exile came to recognize that God was present with them wherever they lived and that there were ways to worship God without a temple.

New covenant: A new and deeper relationship and agreement between God and the people of God. This idea was expressed in one of Jeremiah's messages when he promised that the people would return from exile back to Jerusalem. The new agreement would not have to be memorized; it would be written on the hearts of the people.

Samaritans: People of mixed blood, partially Hebrew and partially of other "races." They were descendants of mixed marriages dating back to the Assyrian conquest of the Northern Kingdom. The Assyrians had deliberately mixed people of different nations to destroy national identities and reduce the possibility of rebellions. When Jews returned from exile in Babylon, they found Samaritans ready to help them rebuild the Temple and the walls of Jerusalem. Many Jews from the Exile had struggled to keep their religion and race pure while in Babylon. They resisted help from Samaritans, who were not of a biologically pure heritage. Resentment increased through the years between Samaritans and Jews. By Jesus' time Samaritans were socially unacceptable to most Jews, although their religious beliefs were quite similar.

Meet Your Bible — AND DISCOVER LIFE

Marker 5 • A PEOPLE WITH A MESSIAH
(Immanuel: God With Us)

4 B.C.–A.D. 30—Jesus

(Note: See Chapter 4 for ideas of **Messiah** and **Christ**.)

"In the beginning. . . .": God is the creator of all creation, including the beginning itself. The opening words of Genesis are repeated as the opening words of John's Gospel. In the first chapter of Genesis, God calls every aspect of creation into being and declares it good. This idea of the goodness of creation is basic to Hebrew and Christian understanding. John declares further that not only did God create the physical world, God also entered the world as a living physical person in Jesus Christ.

In biblical times, and in our day, some religions have taught that the physical world is bad or evil and that only that which is spiritual is good. Both Judaism and Christianity affirm creation, including our physical bodies, to be created by God and therefore good. (*To explore further*, see Genesis 1:1–2:3; Matthew 1:18–2:12; Luke 1:26-56; 2:1-21; John 1:1-5, 14-18.)

Kingdom of God or **Kingdom of heaven:** The reign of God. Jesus told what life is like when persons recognize that God is the reigning power in their lives. Remember what we said in Chapter 4: *The Kingdom was, is, and will be one over which God reigns. The Kingdom is built on love and humility rather than power and might.* While God is all powerful, God gives persons the freedom to accept (or reject) the invitation to live under God's reign.

At points Jesus describes the Kingdom as present; at other points, Jesus talks about the Kingdom as if it is arriving or yet to come. Partly this remains a mystery. We can say, however, that the Kingdom has not fully arrived; much of the world does not recognize God's rule and reign. Even those who claim to be committed Christians fail to live every moment as if living under God's reign. At the same time we do discover those moments when we get a glimpse of what it is like when our lives and our relationships with others and with God are those of the Kingdom. (*To explore further*, see Matthew 5:1-12; 20:1-16; 25:31-46; Luke 8:1-21; 17:20-21.)

Chapter 5   The WHAT of the Bible

Love: Deep care and concern for one or more persons. The New Testament uses two words that are translated as "love" in most English versions. One word is *philos*, which is "brotherly love" (as in Philadelphia) or the friendship type of love. The other word is *agape*, which is the deepest, most self-giving love, which Jesus has shown to his followers. It is the kind of love we find in John 3:16 ("For God so *loved* [italics added] the world. . . ."): God's love for us in sending Jesus Christ, and the love Jesus demonstrated for us on the cross. It is the love Jesus asked his followers to have for one another:

> This is my commandment, that you love one another as I have loved you. No one has greater love than this, to lay down one's life for one's friends. (John 15:12-13)

It was this kind of love that Jesus put above the law and that justified his healing persons and forgiving sins on the sabbath.

Incarnation: God entering the world "in the flesh" in the person of Jesus Christ. (See "In the beginning. . . .") As we have seen, John's Gospel uses symbolic and philosophical language to describe Jesus coming to us in human form. The Gospels of Matthew and Luke give more visual descriptions of Jesus' birth.

The idea of Jesus living in the flesh like one of us goes beyond his birth. It includes how he lived and showed us how to live—and the fact that God knows what it is like to live with all the ups and downs of life in this world. In Jesus, God lived "with us" and experienced every aspect of human life from birth through death—a painful death.

Pharisees: A religious group or sect that tried to apply the law to every situation. Their intentions were good, but many of them focused on the detailed interpretations of the law rather than the spirit and intent of the law. For example, they got upset when Jesus healed people on the sabbath, because Pharisees interpreted that to mean working on the sabbath. Jesus and the Pharisees were often at odds over such issues. The Pharisees saw Jesus as a threat to the law.

Sadducees: A religious group or party that might be characterized as the "establishment" or aristocracy. They disagreed with the Pharisees' picky attention to detail and with the Pharisees' belief in a resurrection of the dead. Many did agree with the Pharisees, however, in seeing Jesus as a threat to their religious life and particularly to the status they held.

Crucifixion: Execution on a cross. When Christians refer to *the* Crucifixion, they are referring to the crucifixion of Jesus. This was a Roman form of execution. The New Testament describes how religious leaders and Roman authorities conspired to have Jesus killed because they saw him as a threat to their authority or to the established way of doing things. (*To explore further*, see Matthew 26–27; Mark 14–15; Luke 22–23; and/or John 18–19.)

Resurrection: Jesus' return and physical appearance to his followers (disciples) after his death. (*To explore further*, see Matthew 28; Mark 16; Luke 24; and John 20–21.)

Marker 6 • *A PEOPLE WITH A MISSION*
(The Journey Continues... Into All the World) The Christian Church

Church: The people of God who recognize Jesus as the Christ and who seek to continue his ministry. The church seeks to live under the guidance of the Holy Spirit. (See Chapter 4 for the explanation of Pentecost and the founding of the church.) People were the church when they *gathered* in someone's home to remember Jesus Christ, to celebrate his life, death, and resurrection, and to support one another in faithful living and ministry to others. They were also the church when they were *scattered* in their daily living and as they continued the ministry and work of Christ. (*To explore further*, see Acts 2:43-47; 1 Corinthians 1:1-17; 16:1-24.)

Chapter 5 — The WHAT of the Bible

Body of Christ: The church is Christ's body on earth called to do Christ's ministry on earth until his return. Paul gave and explained the description in his Letter to the Romans:

> Just as each of us has one body with many members, and these members do not all have the same function, so in Christ we who are many form one body, and each member belongs to all the others.
> (Romans 12:4-5, NIV)[2]

Paul used that description in even greater detail in 1 Corinthians 12:12-26.

REFLECTION TIME: *One Body*

Recall for a moment the different times we have talked about the *people of God*. Remember the call to Abraham and Sarah. Give special attention to what it meant to *become a people* during the Exodus journey with Moses. With all their problems, they had to depend on one another—and God—if they were to survive. The same was true later if they were to survive during the Exile. Being a *people* means more than several individuals who are in the same place at the same time. Something molds them *together* into a *body* that has a life of its own. (It's like the difference between five individuals standing on a basketball court with each bouncing a different basketball and a team that plays together with one ball.)

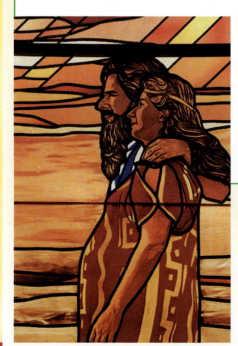

When have you experienced being *part of the body of Christ*? In your group? in your congregation? in gatherings of Christians of different denominations? How can you continue to see yourself as part of that body.

64   **Meet Your Bible**   AND DISCOVER LIFE

Mission: To tell everyone everywhere in the world about Jesus Christ. This is the mission of the people of God who are the church. It is the mission that led a few groups of Jewish followers in Palestine to reach across the world of their day. They also reached across the boundaries of "race" to include Gentiles.

Other points to reflect on: If the early church had not taken its mission seriously, how would you have heard about Jesus Christ? What is your mission as part of the body of Christ today?

[1] Taken from the HOLY BIBLE, NEW INTERNATIONAL VERSION © 1973, 1978 by the International Bible Society, used by permission of Zondervan Bible Publishers.
[2] Taken from the HOLY BIBLE, NEW INTERNATIONAL VERSION.

CHAPTER 6

The SO WHAT of the Bible

It may sound brash to ask "So what?" of the Bible, but the Bible invites and encourages bold questions. When we bring our bold questions, however, we must be open to discovering answers that may lead us in new directions. It does make a difference if we *ask* "So what?" rather than *declare* "So what!" If we are *asking* and *open*, we are ready to take the next steps in a lifetime journey with the Bible.

So What Difference Does It Make for My Life?

Let's visit each marker one more time and explore some of the ways the biblical story has something to do with our lives as the people of God today. You will recognize some of the biblical people, events, and ideas. We will also discover some new parts of the story.

Marker 1 • THE DREAM

(The Journey Begins)
2000 B.C.: Abraham, Sarah, and a Promise

God's Call to a Journey to Make Real the Dream

When we first looked at Marker 1, we talked about God's call to Abraham and Sarah to begin and continue a journey.

By now you may have discovered that God often calls people on journeys. Looking across each marker we see many people God called to take journeys. Parts of some journeys have been the literal distances that could be measured in miles. But even more dramatic have been the parts of the journeys to new situations that had never been explored before. Abraham and Sarah not only traveled great distances, but also had to trust God's promise when all common sense made it seem foolish. Even they had trouble trusting God's promise of having a child as they got older and older. (See Genesis 18:1-15; 21:1-7.)

Meet Your Bible   AND DISCOVER LIFE

For You to Explore Further

At each marker there are other calls to other journeys. Each journey included a vision—God's plan. That vision at first seemed like a dream—something both exciting and not yet real. Some we have mentioned before; some we have not. Check out some of these examples:

God called Moses even when Moses didn't feel adequate for the job. (Marker 2) See Exodus 3:1-15; 4:10-17.

Elijah had faithfully followed God's directions and had been an instrument for God's miracles. Elijah had already faced some risks; but when Queen Jezebel threatened his life, that was too much! He fled into the wilderness, but Elijah could not run away from God. This time God called him in a very quiet way, but called him to some more tasks. (Marker 4) See 1 Kings 19:9-16.

God called Isaiah to be a prophet through a dramatic vision in the Temple. (Markers 3 and 4) See Isaiah 6:1-8.

God called Jeremiah to be a prophet despite Jeremiah's protest that he was too young. (Marker 4) See Jeremiah 1:4-8.

Through Jesus, God called Simon Peter and others to be disciples. (Marker 5) See Matthew 4:18-22; Mark 1:16-20; and/or Luke 5:1-11.

Paul was on a trip to persecute Christians when God, through the risen Jesus, converted Paul. In that conversion was also God's call for Paul's mission and ministry. Note that the fulfillment of Paul's calling depended on other "supporting actors" (Ananias and Barnabas) responding to God's call. (Marker 6) See Acts 9:1-30.

REFLECTION TIME: How is God calling you?

Is God calling you in a dramatic way? in a quiet way? through a worship experience at church? through others? through the talents God has given you?

Is God calling you on a journey that means sitting next to someone in the cafeteria who has no friends? (Perhaps God is calling you first to ask one or two other members of the body of Christ to join you in sitting next to that someone in the cafeteria.)

Is God calling you on a journey to help others build or repair a home for someone who cannot do it for himself or herself?

Is God calling you to a lifetime vocation that may take years of training to develop the talents God has already given you?

What is God calling your group or congregation to be and to do?

Marker 2 • BECOMING A PEOPLE
(The Greatest Camping Trip Ever)
1250 B.C.: Moses and Exodus

Living in the Wilderness (Desert)

The people of God had become slaves in Egypt. The demands of their taskmasters became more and more unbearable. God guided Moses to free the people from oppression. Eventually they would enter the Promised Land, but for a long time they had to wander in the *wilderness*. (The CEV, NIV, and TEV generally use the word *desert*.)

When the going got rough, many of the Hebrews questioned Moses' leadership and whether freedom was worth the price. They declared that as slaves they had adequate food in Egypt, but now Moses had brought them to the wilderness to die of hunger (Exodus 16:1-12) and of thirst (Exodus 17:1-7).

Meet Your Bible   AND DISCOVER LIFE

Time and again God provided for the essential needs of the people. God took care of the people and proved to be trustworthy. Yet the people made and worshiped the golden calf (Exodus 32:1-10) at the very moment Moses was receiving the stone tablets that commanded faithfulness to God.

For You to Explore Further

The idea of *wilderness* or *desert* is used throughout the Bible. Often it is a specific memory of the Exodus. Even when it is a more general reference, there is still a picture of a desolate area that catches our imagination.

Psalm 78 gives a poetic way of remembering the Exodus experience. See Psalm 78:10-20.

Psalm 102 is an individual's prayer for help in a time of trouble. The psalmist feels "like a lonely owl in the desert" (verse 6, CEV). (The NRSV uses "wilderness.") Read the whole psalm. Note the opening of the prayer in verses 1-2; then the description of how the psalmist felt in verses 3-11 (a personal experience that is itself like a desert or wilderness experience). Finally, note how the prayer ends in praise with trust in God's power in verses 12-28.

Immediately after his baptism Jesus went into the wilderness. Like his human ancestors he was tempted to put his trust in choices other than God. How was his response different from theirs? Read Matthew 4:1-11 and/or Luke 4:1-13.

REFLECTION TIME: What does wilderness mean to you?

Does it mean desolate area? desert land? scarce water? uncertain boundaries?

How welcome would water feel to your mouth or to your feet after walking for miles across such an area, wearing sandals?

Are there times in your life when you have experienced *wilderness* situations, either physically or emotionally?

In what idols were you tempted to trust? How difficult was it to remain faithful to God?

What assurance did you have of God's presence?

Marker 3 • A PEOPLE, A LAND, AND A NATION

(When the Act Was All Together)
1000 B.C.: David's United Kingdom

When We've Got It "All Together"

The people finally had it made! They were a people with a land and they had become a great nation. David as king had led the nation to greatness. His name would go down in history. But, as we have seen, David abused the power God had given him. At the very moment his life might have seemed so "all together," David would lose his perspective and let everything fall apart.

Then Solomon, David's son, became king. On the one hand, things seemed even more together with him than under David. Solomon's wisdom is talked about to this day. Solomon also built the Temple.

But Solomon, too, lost his perspective. He tried to do things the way kings of other countries did. He built great stables for vast numbers of horses and chariots. Not only did he marry many foreign wives to forge political deals, he also let his love for them sway him to worship their gods. What had seemed to be the kingdom's greatest moment was the beginning of its falling apart.

Meet Your Bible   AND DISCOVER LIFE

For You to Explore Further

Although the kingdom split after Solomon's death, the leaders and people of both kingdoms again and again allowed their own pride and comfort to direct their attention to themselves rather than to God. Prophets would warn of the disastrous consequences, but were often ignored.

Solomon's wisdom is often remembered with a famous story of two women who claimed the same baby. See 1 Kings 3:16-28.

Solomon had the Temple built in Jerusalem. See 1 Kings 6.

God reminded Solomon to keep his priorities straight. See 1 Kings 9.

Solomon disobeyed God's directions. See 1 Kings 11.

Jeremiah was but one of many prophets who warned the people what would happen because they had their priorities wrong. See Jeremiah 11:15-17.

> **REFLECTION TIME: Can you recall a time when things seemed "so right," but were in reality "so wrong"?**
>
> How can people get their priorities wrong when they seem to "have it all"? What happens to their relationship with God?
>
> What has happened when you have been tempted to put your priorities in the wrong order? How has God reminded you that things could fall apart?

Marker 4 • THE PEOPLE FIND NEW HOPE; RELIGION FINDS NEW FORMS

(When Hebrews Became Jews)
586–538 B.C.: Exile and Return

When We Have to Live in Exile

The nation did not get its priorities in order; it did not live in faithful obedience to God. Thus Judah and its capital, Jerusalem, fell to Babylon. The leading citizens were carried away to Babylon and into captivity. As we saw in Chapter 4, they were treated rather well as exiles. They could own land, plant gardens, and even hold minor political offices. But there were big questions:

If Babylon conquered Judah did it mean that the gods of the Babylonians were mightier than the God of Judah?

Was God with them in Babylon or was God still back in Judah? Was it possible for God to be in both places at once?

How could they worship God without the Temple? Not only was it back in Jerusalem, it was also in ruins.

Could they survive as the people of God? Could they keep their identity or would they be absorbed as part of the Babylonian population?

Meet Your Bible — AND DISCOVER LIFE

Guidance from prophets like Jeremiah and Ezekiel helped the people learn how to live as *the people of God in exile*. That meant to live in tension between two worlds. They worked and lived as responsible citizens in Babylon, but their first loyalty was to God and their first citizenship was as the people of God. Because their loyalties were different, *they were different* from their neighbors. They worshiped at different times and in different ways from their neighbors. Many scholars believe that the Jewish synagogue began during the Exile as a place to gather, to offer prayers, and to learn and pass on the traditions.

For You to Explore Further
The people in exile received help in how to live and how to live faithfully from prophets like Jeremiah and Ezekiel. Jeremiah wrote a letter from Jerusalem to the exiles. Ezekiel was a member of the first group taken into exile.

After explaining why he wrote the letter, Jeremiah gave the details of the letter. It opened by telling the people how to live as good citizens in exile. See Jeremiah 29:1-7.

Jeremiah warned the people about fortune tellers and false prophets who would raise unrealistic hopes of an early return home to Jerusalem. See Jeremiah 29:8-9.

Jeremiah did offer hope of a return to Jerusalem and of a restored relationship with God. See Jeremiah 29:10-14.

Ezekiel had several dramatic visions with important messages for the people. One message of hope was given through the vision of the valley of dry bones. See Ezekiel 37:1-14.

REFLECTION TIME: How and when do you live in exile?
When have you found yourself living in tension between two worlds? What is it like to be different because your loyalties and priorities are different from those of the crowd around you?

When you are in exile from your homeland, how do you sing the Lord's song in the foreign land? What gives you hope?

Marker 5 • *A PEOPLE WITH A MESSIAH*
(Immanuel: God With Us)
4 B.C.–A.D. 30: Jesus

Christ Comes Into Our Lives

Jesus Christ came into the world to restore our broken relationship with God. In other words, Christ forgives us.

We have not used the word *sin* very much in this book, but we have talked about it a lot. When we talked about the disobedience and unfaithfulness of the people of God in the wilderness, we were talking about sin. When we talked about David's abuse of power, we were talking about sin. *Sin occurs when we reject God's will and way and insist on our own.*

If God lived by the letter of the agreement with Abraham or Moses, the relationship would have been over very early in the story. God never even said, "Three strikes and you're out!" God kept offering the people of God forgiveness and new chances to renew their relationship with God.

Then God took an even more dramatic step and came into the world as a human being. Jesus experienced everything we experience: birth, growing up, friends who help you, friends who abandon you, friends who betray you; and finally, he experienced death. In all he did, Jesus both *taught* and *showed* people how to live.

Jesus was more than a teacher and an example. He came into the lives of the people of God. He came to restore the relationship the people could not keep.

Again, however, the people rejected the relationship and this greatest show of God's love. They wanted their way over God's way.

For You to Explore Further

The tragic news is that when we talk about the people of God who choose their way over God's way, we are talking about us. We are the people today who want it all our way. The good news is that God does not give up on us. Human words are never adequate when we try to talk about God and what God does. That is why the New Testament helps by using several different ways to talk about God's love and the relationship God continues to offer us.

Jesus talked about God's love that keeps reaching out to us. To make his point he told about *a lost sheep*, *a lost coin*, and *two lost sons*. The story of the two lost sons is sometimes called "The Prodigal Son." Why, do you think, were there really two lost sons? See Luke 15.

The very title of this book emphasizes that Jesus came to bring *life* to those who believe. Jesus also talked in terms of being the *light* in a world that prefers darkness. See John 3:16-21.

Paul uses different words to talk about how Christ restores our broken relationship with God. We cannot overcome our sin that has broken the relationship, but Christ can and does overcome that sin and brokenness. That healed relationship is a gift that we accept in faith. See Romans 5:1-11.

The relationship with God is one of love. If we grasp what that love means, then we extend that love to others. See 1 John 4:7-21.

REFLECTION TIME: What are the words and word pictures that best describe your relationship with God? with Jesus Christ?
How have you experienced brokenness, hurt, forgiveness, and acceptance in relationships with family and close friends? What barriers had to be overcome to restore a relationship that you had broken?

How is our relationship with God like other relationships? How is our relationship with God different from all other relationships?

How does Jesus Christ make our relationship with God different? How does Christ make our relationships with other people different?

Meet Your Bible — AND DISCOVER LIFE

Marker 6 • *A PEOPLE WITH A MISSION*

(The Journey Continues . . . Into All the World)
The Christian Church

Our Lap on the Journey

With Jesus' life, death, and resurrection, God offered a new covenant built on a love so great that we will never fully understand it. It is a love that changed frightened disciples into courageous missionaries. It is a love that propelled those disciples from the security of a locked room out into a diverse world to boldly proclaim the good news of God's love in Jesus Christ. It is a love that reached out—and reaches out—to "unchosen people" and makes them "chosen."

This is where our lap of the journey begins: the "unchosen" made "chosen." Unless you are of one hundred percent Jewish blood, *you are one of the "unchosen" who has become "chosen."* Whether many generations back, one generation back, or if you are the first in your family, God's call reached you through the mission of the church. And now you are the church!

Don't let the strange twists of the journey confuse you. God used the first Christians, who were Jews, to reach out to the "unchosen" Gentiles and then made them "chosen." *So the church is basically "unchosen" people who have become "chosen" people of God.*

Now we are called to reach out to those who are still "unchosen." We are called to let the "unchosen" discover that God's love reaches out to *choose* them. This is our lap on the journey of the people of God.

A friendly warning! We can be as disobedient and unfaithful as other people of God on their laps of the journey. We can fool ourselves by acting as if being "chosen" was something we accomplished. We can take such pride in being "chosen" that we ignore God's call to reach out to the "unchosen" on our street, in our school, and around the world.

Like the Hebrew prophets we need to remind one another that the church is not a club for a select few. The church is made up of "unchosen" people who have become "chosen" and sinners who are forgiven.

For You to Explore Further

The risen Lord appeared to the disciples several times. He calmed their fears, responded to doubts, and directed them to continue his ministry. Jesus promised and empowered the disciples with the Holy Spirit for that ministry.

The Holy Spirit appeared at Pentecost, marking the birth of the church. The church—the people of God—struggled to be faithful as it faced persecutions, temptations, and difficult decisions.

After his resurrection, Jesus appeared to the disciples. After responding to their fears and doubts, he directed the disciples to proclaim his message in Jerusalem and from there to every nation. See Luke 24:36-49.

The disciples had been living in fear when Jesus appeared to empower them with the Holy Spirit and to send them out in ministry. See John 20:19-23.

Thomas was absent when the risen Jesus first appeared in the room to the disciples. He was skeptical when the others told him about seeing Jesus. Jesus appeared again to respond to Thomas' doubts. See John 20:24-29.

Peter, like the other disciples, tried to live as both a faithful Jew and a follower of Christ. For Peter that meant avoiding certain kinds of food considered unclean. Likewise, he would have considered Gentiles to be unclean in religious dealings. God challenged Peter with a vision and with a call to go to Cornelius, a Roman military officer. See Acts 10.

Paul had a special calling as a missionary to the Gentiles. He made several journeys through the Mediterranean world, establishing and giving guidance to churches both through his visits and through his letters. See Acts 16:4-10; 20:17-38; Romans 15:14-21; Galatians 1:11–2:10.

> **REFLECTION TIME: What does it feel like to be "unchosen"? How does it feel to be "chosen" after being "unchosen"?**
>
> Can you recall what it was like to be one of the last ones chosen for a team at school? Or maybe when some of your friends were going someplace but did not invite you?
>
> How does it feel to be chosen for a major responsibility because someone believes in you and appreciates your gifts and skills?
>
> Who and where are the unchosen persons God has called you to tell that they are chosen?

Chapter 6 — The SO WHAT of the Bible

NOTES